REAL

'A wonderful meditation on the language of grief, want, lust, and hope. Thomas Stewart's poems show how barbs of strength emerge after plucking away all thorns, then allowing them to regrow'

JENNI FAGAN

'A beautiful and wistful collection which wrangles with life's ample grief and heartache. Stewart captures the delicate balance of queerness and masculinities, highlighting how we so often mythologise our fathers even when they have capacity to cause great anguish after death. These poems have immortalised his father and serve as a place of returning, a lyrical gravestone to make sense of the senseless'

ANDRÉS N. ORDORICA

'These poems are a revelation. Traversing grief, masculinity, and some of my favourite pop-culture moments. I took great comfort from Thomas Stewart's collection'

LOTTE JEFFS

ABOUT THE AUTHOR

Based in Edinburgh, Thomas Stewart studied at the University of South Wales and creative writing at the University of Warwick. In 2021, he was awarded a New Writers Award from the Scottish Book Trust where he was mentored by Claire Askew. In 2020, he was Highly Commended in the Verve Poetry Competition, and his poem was included in the anthology, *We've Done Nothing Wrong, We've Nothing to Hide* (Verve Poetry Press, 2020). Thomas is the author of two poetry pamphlets: *Based on a True Story* (fourteen poems, 2022) and *Empire of Dirt* (Red Squirrel Press, 2019), a Poetry Book Society selection.

To Claire →

With gratitude.

REAL BOYS

Thomas Stewart

T. Stewart

Polygon

First published in paperback in Great Britain in 2024 by Polygon, an imprint of
Birlinn Ltd | West Newington House | 10 Newington Road| Edinburgh | EH9 1QS

9 8 7 6 5 4 3 2 1

www.polygonbooks.co.uk

ISBN 978 1 84697 667 4
eBook ISBN 978 1 78885 677 5

British Library Cataloguing-in-Publication Data
A catalogue record for this book is available from the British Library.

The publisher acknowledges support from the National Lottery through
Creative Scotland towards the publication of this title.

Typeset in Verdigris MVB by The Foundry, Edinburgh
Printed and bound in Great Britain by Clays Ltd, Elcograf S.p.A.

MIX
Paper | Supporting
responsible forestry
FSC
www.fsc.org
FSC® C018072

This book is dedicated to my father
James Gordon Stewart
1953–2016

CONTENTS

GIVE ME MY GRIEF BACK

let me hold it like a lizard in my hand

choose to throw it from my grasp
when I've had enough of it
crawling across my palm

let me sleep with my grief
smell its milky morning dew
wipe the crust from its eyes

let it be mine
to wear like a
dirty moth-eaten coat

let me write a poem and pluck it
like a leaf from a branch
then burn it in among the lilies

let me walk away from my grief
if only to know it is walking behind
and I am leading

only then will I
plant my grief in the ground
and watch it grow as a tree

only then will I see
some kind of life form
from this death

BOTANOPHOBIA

I have always been
a fearful person:

scared of climbing
trees, scared
of the dark, of the sharp
edge of a cactus, of
the growth of plants –
scared of their whispers,
and seeds, scared
of their invisible,
beating hearts.

I once ate a seed;
my mother said
a plant would grow
in my stomach –
I curled over
the toilet,
my vomit
looked like
rose petals,
it smelt of the
Radyr hawkweeds,
red clovers,
ragged-robins
and meadow
buttercups
that congregated

in my
grandfather's
garden.

THERE ARE BEES IN MY BEARD

and they don't even have the decency
to sting me.
They drag their blades across the skin
not hacking out a single hair.

The bees drop honey in my eyes
and their milky eggs in my ears
so I can't hear their conspiracy.

I am filled with the bees' nectar.
I am their home,
their front doors, their windows.

I wake one day to no eggs in my ears
or honey in my eyes
or bees in my beard –
with no bee-stings to remember them by.

CONKERS

When I smashed the conkers
and laid them out,
when I felt their broken
pieces and gathered them up,
when I smelt the vinegar
of their cracked shells
and wanted to take them home
I thought of the head boy:
red-haired Einstein,
most likely to succeed,
went into the woods
behind the gym one day
with only meth
and a can of Seven Up
and a photo of his mum
and a long rope.
Beyond the tennis courts we heard
the police shout: *Cut him down!*
with voices like flower vases
shattering.

When I left the conkers
and walked home
to pass a bridge
covered in ivy
I saw that boy
who tried to jump off the edge
but was stopped by a stranger,
I saw that dangling boy

in literal limbo
and heard the voices
of the others boys
shouting: *Gay boy, faggot.*
And when the boy abandoned
the bridge,
his mother hid the pills
and all the belts
were locked
in Ikea boxes,
and the house became
a safe space.
The boy found a box-cutter
when his mother
was at work.

When I walked through the park
and leaves wondered
with me,
I couldn't remember
the name of the girl
that everyone forgot,
that filled herself
with her grandma's
paracetamol and sat between
the goalposts.
They found her in the morning,
a dog walker or near enough,
and the newspaper clipping

was short and un-sweet –
just kept calling her *girl*.

When I slept that night
on a wooden bed
I could smell the conkers
in the feathers of the
pillow, I could hear their
song in my dreams,
I could feel them broken
yet protruding
through the springs
of the mattress.

LEVIATHAN

When I was a baby, a leviathan stole me into the sea.
My big sister dropped her shopping bags and dived
into that dirty water; head-first, not knowing
if she'd open her skull on a rock before she got to me,
she just dived, determined and screaming. When she found
me, I was playing cards with that creature,
taking spades from its tentacles, clubs from its teeth.
I remember her there, underwater, out of breath,
frowning at me. How could I befriend this beast? This thing
she didn't understand, this other she'd been taught to fear,
taught to keep her baby brother away from?

FIRST SIGN
(or Stone Man)

I see the moon: quiet above our table at the restaurant on the seafront.

I think of the ocean quivering when my father coughed and very
       suddenly

went down, his head hit the table and it seemed everything froze

like dust in sunlight.

I hear the wind returning after my mother steeled in her terror, stood

and brought my father back from the dead, after his breath came thick

like the tumble from a cliffside.

Just like something that ancient and invincible, my father waved off the
       incident –

fine all fine – sipped his beer. Everyone was quick to forget.

But the blood in my veins had changed direction.

I stood on the beach and watched the ocean devour the moon;

went back to the villa and lay beneath the fan cutting the air

and felt my body ring with stone.

THE WIZARD OF OZ

When the tornado refused to come,
I dug a hole in the ground,
pushed my face into the earth
and appeared
some place in colour.

TOBACCO

stop lighting up in the car flicking your ash out of the window into my
        window
onto my suit so I'm ash-stained for the wedding *smelling like a brawl*
        my aunt says

I hide your cigarettes around the house not a treasure hunt you're
        interested in
but angry at – *don't give me a map give me co-ordinates details a location*

you just get a new packet of Lambert & Butler before the day of
        diseased bodies
beneath the label I badgered you about all that wasted money those
        plunged lungs

at some point I reconcile that this is who you'll always be –
I respect your resistance to change

found a holiday spot you liked so we go back every year for four years
finally tasted a tikka masala that tasted right – *we only order from Ema*
        Balti now

and afterwards you banish yourself to the kitchen and the columns of
        smoke seep
under the doors and the smell of you follows me to university to the
        smokers' room

no thanks I don't smoke, I say before taking a drag that becomes a
        scavenger hunt
every drunken night not a smoker if I don't own a packet

a packet of Lambert & Butler I say on the day I buy my first pack –
a sigil of our house

*   *   *

while making a film the air smelling of old wet pages I get a call
take it in a corridor which seems familiar seems like bad news

told you have cancer
no peppered jargon like in the films no stage this months that just
            cancer that's all you have

*   *   *

in the hospital you want a fag and the word stings but you don't mean
            it that way –
just impatient in the bed ignorant of your weaknesses and petulance

waiting for mum, Jen, a nurse, someone familiar to care for
you don't want your baby boy to take you to the toilet wheelchair
            outside anywhere

beyond the bed where we realise it will be just us for a while –
something we both feared for a long time –

and we face it in the hospital where I draw a wheelchair
and you look from that to me making a decision finally saying: *let's get
            out of here Tom*

and I hold your hand and you take it
and I place you into the chair and you let me
and I wheel you away from reality
where we aren't afraid of one another

nor lost for words –
there's so much more to fear

PACT

we will not turn on each other

we will not blame the sea or the crab

we will do everything we can
            to protect our parents

to care for our father until he dies

to care for our mother during
and after his death

to care for her always

we are the children of stone
and of air

we will do this
            because we do not speak
                        the language of defeat

stubbornness is a virtue
            not a sin

here are our family mottos
            but

we forget

being a hero
        has its price

POETIC LICENSE

I watched a son
buy a motorbike
the same model,
and colour red,
as his dead father's.
I watched him
a little less lost,
driving off
into the fat,
hot, orange sun.
I watched him
disappear
into a world still
without his father.
I found it incredibly
sad.

I thought I'd write
a poem about it
and thought
it wasn't my poem
to write.
I did not have the right
to tell this story,
I was not
this son,
it was not my red
motorbike,
not my dead father.

I thought
I had no right
to this story;
I did not belong
to it, I was a spectator,
I was copper,
I was the bronze
blistering sun,
I was the mountain,
I was the scattered
brown purpling stones.

I thought what license,
what connection,
what bond but blood
did I share
with my own father.
I thought
I had no motorbike
to buy,
no lost identity
of a man
I did not know
to find,
I had it all right
in front of me
I just kept looking
for a motorbike.

BUILDING A WARDROBE WITH MY FATHER

I've always been shit at DIY.
My experience is primarily in holding shelves,
standing stationary, arms upright, silent
as my father leant into that cramped space
and our faces were so close that I could smell
his skin – boot-strapped, sun-bleached, clad
in iron – I almost reached out
and touched it, the way my mother would
as he lay on the sofa for a nap and she'd squeeze
the spots on his cheek and he'd yelp, protest,
but then lie back and let her, like a cat
allowing the fleas to be plucked. He was submissive
in his own way, found love at the edge of a drill,
telling me to: *Keep still, don't get too close,*
barking at me to watch my fingers, to not hurt myself,
to be safe.

REAL BOY

This is a true story.

They said
you're not a real
boy until you cut
the wizard out of the tree.

It's a question
of which tree:
real boys might pick
oak, birch or beech,
and then boys
that pick alder,
elm or hawthorn
are unreal.

Unreal boys hold the axe
and whisper:
Cousin of Merlin,
give me some magic.

But magic
is not a boy's language,
here, in the boys'
toilets, or there in the
changing rooms, it is
the outstretched branch
welcoming you –

to be a real boy.

Unreal boys, who hide
under their towels
or become black dots
on the rugby pitch

or study the mole
above their nipple,
or the drooping stomach
in the mirror,

are the quietly
hungry trees
in the breeze;

if I were a tree,
I'd be a white willow
by the bay, a *salix
alba* – alone and sexless;
I would only know
the touch of my own
branches.

Yet,
as I long to be
a real boy,
I know I am already
a tree, made of roots,

standing in the wind,
in solitude, exposed,

displaying my chest,
made of wood,
my bushy hair
and eyebrows falling,
falling
past my chipped teeth,

across the scar on my
chin and the leaves
growing from
my hands.

SUNFLOWERS

We stabbed the dirt
with apple seeds,
denting marks in the world's soil,
and when our little, desperate
fingers unhooked,
we desired only to win.

Our seeds created gaunt
drooping things:
these were the heads
of serpents, not sunflowers,
the bodies too slender
and fragile that their faces
spent their time hunching.

We brought them out
of our gardens and stood
them side-by-side;
we poked at the disc flower,
pulled on the sepal and
bract and rays;
the morbid fashion show
ended with the tallest
winner, but it was the seed
planter that got the award,
the earth digger, the world's butcher;
for that sullen sunflower
arched its shoulders
giantly gazing down

tied by thin string
to the wall.

The ugly ones were discarded,
snapped down,
tossed in black bags;
you could've seen it as
a mercy killing
but most of the seed planters
just didn't want to buy
a watering can.

SPACE JAM

The real boys stole my father,
put a basketball in his mouth,
spat adornment at his feet;

they smelled of new PE kits,
Vaseline, Lynx –
I wanted to be them.

Or maybe I tasted
my father's desire
that I give him something to see,

to scalp my hands
and pick up bruises,
speak his language.

*   *   *

When the real boys went home,
I stood beneath the net:
flapping like a flag one pledges allegiance to;

I saw my reflection;

your eyes become my eyes.

I'm sorry, Dad,
I know you loved me anyway.

MAKING LOVE TO A MAN

I've been asking myself this question
for days: what is manly? What is making love,
what is a man? If not a twig upon an old oak,
a lion amongst the others in the den, roaring
loud enough to drown out those attempting
to sing. Is making love to a man similar to
a bear or a lion or some other violent creature,
beautiful in its own way, even with blood
around its mane? If that is the case, then I myself
am a lion or a grizzly with the heart of a lizard,
locking my claws into a crown of thorns,
catching my lover's chest hair between my teeth.
Here, two lions
tangle into serpents and ravens, cats and jellyfish,
all the colours of the world, all the visions of the body
flash in this moment, in this act,
making love
to a man   as a man,   shedding our skins
to the wild
yes,
out
to the wild.

TEETH / DESTRUCTION

I've always hated
the taste of mint,
hated counting
to 120 seconds
staring at myself
in the mirror
letting the tap run.
I hate.
So now I wake
to that grubby plaque,
kiss my man
with smoky morning
breath laced with
Pepsi. I shower
and stare at
my toothbrush,
reach out
and pull away
rejecting
a natural
instinct.
My tooth cracked,
and my father died.
I had another root canal
and the dentist tilted
his head like he was
disappointed in me,
and when he did that
I saw my father.

The dentist held open
my mouth
knocked his gloved hand
against my nose,
attempted
to scrape away
the damage
I'd caused.
I lay there,
looking up
at the light
thinking about ghosts
trying
to say:
Sorry,
sorry,
I'm sorry.

THE MEN WHO WORE FOXES ON THEIR HEADS

I prayed to the moon
that the men who wore foxes on their heads
would leave us alone forever;

that our apple tree
would bloom past midnight.
In return, the moon created a blurry light

enough to see the men who wore foxes on their heads
destroy my mother's garden
and leave ash in the air.

CARDIFF GRINDR, 2015
(or *fuck*)

I don't want to fuck anymore:

no longer walking into stranger's flats, not knowing their faces,
their names;

no longer hunting for the stories or the rush of vodka-blowjobs.
I am no longer full of the desire to fuck and feel numb, fuck and
feel dead; to fuck, not for the orgasm, but to simply fuck and to
be fucked; yet now I long

to be touched, to speak with the man inside me, to lay my head
upon their chest. I am so obliterated, I am a cliché. Like a fallen
chandelier. I am so unready for this new life without, I am
scrambling for intimacy, running the streets stabbed

by lamplight and metallic tangs of beer rolling over my teeth. I
go to his house because he has finally replied, and because with
him, there is someone I feel this affinity towards – blinded by my
own demands – not desire, not love –

but need. After we fuck, he tells me he's seeing someone; he
never says the word cancer, he doesn't ask. When I dare speak of
it, he, like them all, listens as if it's the most normal thing, like
they've heard this story before, it's just one of those things –

everybody dies.

And here, now, I have to nod. For I am dying. This is my death.

My funeral. My crematorium.

Fuck, this is the end for me.

Fuck, this is the end of me.

Some speck at the end of a bar, some smile in a crowd, some tequila chat, blown apart by stars and castles   autonomy immortality   but

everybody dies: I am dying on this pavement, I have walked past my ghost, my dead, my soul, my creator, they have all told me to go on,

go on, get out of here, you're not dead yet.

OESOPHAGUS

someone has planted a tree
in my   oesophagus
leaves in my gut
roots sketching
in my asshole   climbing
through a ladder
of their making   fuck
it must be good
to feel alive, even
though you kill me   tree
you grow

MY FATHER'S BODY

I.

Leg

Your legs look like peaches exploded in a rotting autumn,
a spell without magic. Did you count your steps
before that bed sealed you in? I trapped a spider

under the rim of a jam jar, and accidentally tore off
one of its legs. It hung from the wall
like a deer's head – decapitated

and honoured. I prayed to that leg, like the prayers
I make to your purpling skin, my crucifix,
my amulet, my hope.

II.
Face
(or Death Mask)

gaunt skeletal angular
slack-jawed bag of bones

your skin looks like your elbows
your body like a tooth yellow-aged
mechanical fragile. I feel like

your soul has already tried to leave
and is trapped under a rock
at the bottom of the deepest sea

the place where life locks you in

and what a cruel joke
that life should actually leave you
and death merely touch your fingertip

exhaustion rests behind your eyes
like a teabag drying on a saucer

and all the lines on your face
all your stories and scars begin to fade

III.
Mouth

blistered
like sunburn
flaking

      like the cracking soles of feet
          after a dust walk

dust falling from the curtains
          onto dry lips

dust is dead skin

      there's a lot in this room

I want to wear a tree's skin
      like a coat
          at that realisation

IV.

Feet

dried skin purpling beneath sandal straps
makes me think of our summer holiday in Turkey
and the smell of cigarette smoke in sunlight in the morning
and the sound of the newspaper crackling when you'd flip the page
and how you always sat hunched over bare-chested coughing
your skin falling into snowflakes dissolving before it touched the floor
and those red hot steaks, your feet sometimes purple
with the green vein protruding like a lizard or a tube
your blood nakedly pumping
the smoke coiling lines on the monitor

V.

Nose

Got your nose. The big, bulbus bee in the centre of my face,
your face, the face of family. I did not choose
this face and nor did you yours. I wonder whose nose you had
before snapping it off and placing it in your pocket
beside clumps of dust. I wonder how long you spent in the belly
of the whale, before reappearing, years later,
reshaped, formed by your own hand, anew. But you still had that nose,
the nose you gave to your children, like the rest of you, the eyes,
the fingers, the toes, our very own Geppetto. I envy the whale
whose belly you lay in for years. I envy the way your cheek
would rest against the flesh of the animal; the way your skin peeled off
and attached to the whale's gut. I wish I could haul you up
to ask you questions, at least then, when you died
I would have some notion of you. If I were a whale,
I would make the whole world love me –
before swallowing it whole.

VI.
Hand

They're still on the bed beside you
like I imagine the dead to be

they remind me of basketballs

the way you showed me how to hold them

one hand cradling the side
the other flat like a spider

swish and flick

and you'd always strike
my father the basketball player

who could've played in Canada
had enough life

– been other people –
would you have lived longer there?

When I missed the net you'd gather
all of the little patience within you

then grab my hands and put them
on the basketball: *Like this, like that,*

and I'd swish and I'd flick and I'd miss
and we'd do it all over again –

it never occurred to you
that I just wanted

to hold your hand.

VII.
Voice

My father, the mermaid, lost his voice,

was no longer able to swallow
the sea whole or crack a wave
into six from the back of his throat,

he sounded like the groan of an old house,
words lost in ghosts lost in corridors.

I can't really remember his voice anymore,
just the occasional phrase, but not sentences.

All I have are my memories, blotted now
with the ones where he can't swallow,

where he decays in front of me, where he withers
away. If a dog lost his voice,

if he lay dying before us, we'd end his suffering
but if I were to do the same,

I'd end up in a cell. It would have been worth it,
just so he could die

with a voice.

WIDOW

Her eyes
are rope burns
sobs muffled
by starshined curtains
she is a crescent moon
hiding   in herself
in the dark
on the bed
I go to her give her
what I can   for words
will not suffice

I hold the moon with my ribbon arms
trying to contain
the enormity of her thoughts,
in this moment
she is everything but
and I am not
the boy this story belongs to,

we avoid the words,
we avoid that word,
we're not ready yet.

DEATH CITY

Over the horizon
I found the golden fragments of moons
that were once suns.

Here, hope is stuck
at the edge of a cliff – where
there is no lamplight, no bedtime story, no

countless dreams – there is only today
and the day after, the mourning of
who you once were.

Here, in the stones of a wall, or there
in the spine of a book. You are
as you once were, before

where death did not penetrate this ruin
of flats, this Dunelm wasteland –

you can dream out of a city
that is your deathbed

but can you ever leave?

DECLARATION
after Weekend

of course the declaration of love
          is spoiled
by two lads   shouting: *Faggot*

*   *   *

and they do it to
  feel powerful
   if only for a moment
    to have a laugh
      and to solidify
       their masculine
        heterosexuality
          to avoid the desire
          they have
                to press
           their nose into
            their mate's ear,
             to lick his sweat
              and taste the sea
               to wrap into him
               and breathe

WEEKEND
after Andrew Haigh

I.
Shame

'Straight people like us as long as we conform,
we behave by their little rules.'

I found a home in you
the way a mouse holes up
in the walls,
scurries between dark patches,
steals crumbs at eleven,

but outside, vultures
purring their wings
ready to flock
as I touch your hand,

to watch us
buying tickets
to a queer film –

or something close to queer
something only the queers would see –
like when you asked me
to watch *Sex and the City 2*

and I imagined those wings
growing thick around my neck,

feathers stuffed in my mouth,
down my throat,
locked in my lungs.

Each time I spat one out
another appeared.

II.
Pride

I remember when
my ex-boyfriend said
he hated other gay men.

I was fine, of course,
monogamously sucking his cock,
but the other queens
had to be dethroned.

When we broke up,
he became the figurehead
of pride.

III.

Ghetto

I never fell down a rabbit hole.

In Birmingham
they have a whole village,
my boss said to me,
you'll love it.

And I thought – how many ghettos
make a country?

Let's not upset the straights,
I thought, *let's hide*
in our little ghettos,
let's not hold hands,
let's not kiss in the street.

All this hate
for the men who are finally them,
all this hate for that boy
staring back at me
in the mirror.

I V.

Dad, I'm gay.

Here I am imagining
a future where we talked truth;

here I am muttering
but my Glen has been replaced
with an empty fireplace
covered in fairy lights
littered with peaches
next to a wooden floor
so bare and spacious
that I could fill this space
with all the things I have to say to you
I could pack an entire pamphlet of poems
dedicated to you,

but instead I'll sit alone
drunk from a night of empty conversation
where my grief hangs on a peg
like a coat
left behind
on your first day of school

I'll sit here, alone
with the fireplace and

I'll imagine you're alive

and your eyes are focused
and your cigarette is puffing
a gateway
for me to step through

I'll say: *Dad, I'm gay*
I like guys, not girls

and you could tell me
you're proud of me,
could say: *More proud*
than if I were the first man
on the moon.
But that was never your style,

it would be enough
for you to listen,

enough for you
to keep looking at me.

BURIAL SITE

near the brook – under the pine cones
you'll find the boy I buried

joylessly folding that version
of himself into the dirt

where a cigarette butt is thrown
and a crow wrinkles its wings

atop a place that should've been ours –

if only I hadn't shot a star out of the sky

if only the wood hadn't chanted
an old song better hidden

in the wind picking up her pace
sending waves through my eyes

to the bones holding me up
to the tempest and the snowstorm

to the boy standing
in my grave

PRINCE PWYLL VISITS HIS SON'S GRAVE

You are dead Blue,
snatched before I ever heard your words;

if there's anything to remember, it is
your battle cry breaking as you came into this world.

You, of course, deserved better
than a prince for a father hiding his nakedness

in blood. Whose gifts were decapitated heads,
tongues and iron-honour larynx. You

were my boy-eyed trophy Blue pinned
to my chest and displayed though I never knew

who you were. My pride overrode the fact your face
was left in the wind. If I had simply held you

made more than fire. If I had not gone out
to hunt a wild boar – to kill as a response to birth

blood is blood is blood – if I had broken tradition
started anew brought my baby boy into the world

with this new kind of blooded hand, if I, if I, if –
is it arrogance to say you wouldn't be here in this grave?

IVAN THE TERRIBLE AND HIS SON

What did you do? What
did you just do?

Cradling his crippled head,
holding onto him now

so tightly, far more tightly
than when he were alive –

your blood is his blood,
between your fingers –

no matter how hard you try
to close the hole in his head –

his blood is your blood –

that body, limp in your arms;
you made, you ended

that hole, the final blow
you delivered

to a body you constantly tried
to pack and unpack,

dismantle and re-establish
his head screwed into

the wrong places,
twisted, contorted, broken.

DEAD STAR

Nuclear ekes out
& a star dies;

coronas fall, ignite,
supernovas crash, neutron stars
set the galaxies alight –

the collapsed star swirls
in that still pacific dusk,
gliding

masses close together
a black hole breathes life.

*   *   *

The dead folk live in the stars,
my mother told me
when there was no one
to look for.

If dead folk live in the stars,
then the stars are watching.
There's something to that –
if I'm lonely, I look up,

and I see that unreadable light,
my death stars staring, wordless,
knowing the answers now –

I envy their truce.

*   *   *

Discussing

who   will   carry   him

        deciding

        where   to have our   last

                        memories

                deciphering

        which   coffin   to have:

                                brown or black
                                wooden or wicker
                                modern or old

                there are no stars
                in coffins, no light
                to guide your way,

                selecting

        food   venue   who will do what

I stood in the car park
and shouted about
that venue –

he deserves better than
                    a goddamn
            rugby club
        with
a goddamn metal fucking fence

            sorting

out   what   to do with his clothes

            too soon to do it
            and too late not to,
            somewhere we believe
            he'll come back

                        we'll blink
                        and it's forgotten

            writing

my   father's   eulogy,

            collecting

memories   like stones

*   *   *

writing about my father
        in the past tense,

                how do I say

                        what I want to say?
                        How do I paint
                        a picture
                        without lying?

      I write *he*
      was, said, did,
      used, went, would,

      past not present,
      walked, smoked,
      laughed, willed,
      ed, ed, ed, ed,

there is is   no   future   tense   anymore

                *   *   *

             returning

      to   the house   when there's nothing left

to organise, no funeral to prepare, no suits to wear

now what?

*   *   *

a red dwarf star
can live up to a hundred
billion years,
it will knit old
pieces back together,

it will outlive
the universe.

BURNING MY FATHER'S PJS

(an omen)

the end of the joint touches
the pyjamas I chose for him –

something warm,
he was always cold, something
warm I now wear in winter,
something warm stained
with ash –

it is an omen.

HALF ORPHAN

We burnt the bridge
        from opposite ends
                at birth-break,

and shouted our adjectives
        for grief across the smoke.
The fires

of our dead burnt higher,
so we returned sympathy
                with ash.

GLADIATOR(S)

and with the pact broken
        like seashells flecked
                on shores from bullet waves

then came the silence filling the hallways
                the empty spaces left
on the sofa: we didn't know how

to hold

each other

and then that rumble
        from the frosty hills
                that quiver

spray-painted in tinsel and in dust

the Colosseum was lit, candles blinked

and in the most simple
        of sentences
                after a laugh and a glass of wine

        something seemingly harmless

there's just one thing I can't
forgive

and first blood is spilled

SISTER ACT II

Do you know what I hate most
     about you being dead?

There's nothing I can pick up
     and throw.

DEAD TOOTH

my dead tooth is deadlocked in my gum under my nose
there's a sparrow on a chippered block
maybe I've smoked too much pot tonight
because I'm thinking of yellow roads
and curled blue grey dead toes
no it's rot it's black and purple and heartbroken red
it's bottles of dried paint and cracked brush tips
this dead tooth is making me dizzy
and disillusioned and mopey
the Oscars is on and Renée Zellweger Judy Garland
is saying heroes and I think chocolate
and the sound of sweets unwrapping like sheets during sex
there's a storm tonight and I'm trying to concentrate on that
I've been up since five on a bus for eleven hours but I'm awake
I'm alive even though
I carry this dead thing round with me
like a parcel with no address
like aching muscles'
dead weight

AND THEN THE FLOWERS CAME

Draw
the curtains, close
the shutters, lock
the windows –

I don't
want to see

outside
the trees can
smell me, their
roots
brew plots,
they're watching
me, with
everyone else

my neighbour
is a part
of the hibiscus
across
the road,
she watches
how many cigarettes
I smoke
or how many times
I check Grindr
on my phone

she looks
around my shoulder
like Eden's viper,
the wind taunts,
the clouds move
without asking –

so close it all up, let
me throw the duvet
over my head, let
me block out
the sound of sunlight
and the heat
of dandelion-clocks,
let me die
here, in the darkness.

And
when everyone has
vanished,
given up,
gone home,
they come.

MY ANXIETY LIVES AS AN ACORN IN MY STOMACH

My anxiety lives as an acorn in my stomach, like a reminder;

a cold, almost silent, whisper. It will always be there.
    We've met and can never un-meet.

        'You will never get rid of me,' it likes to say.
        'I'm part of you now.'

My anxiety is a physical memory
    of the circumstances into which we met. It is a time
        traveller,
        both locking me in and sending me into the
        past.
    It is a kaleidoscope of my worst horrors, old worries
        and tired pain.
    It is small, now, smaller than it once was. Sometimes,
the acorn shrivels
to the size of a seed. But I am aware it can always grow again. My
    guts are the dirt
        into which it blossoms.

*   *   *

This is foreign. One week,
        deep in November,
    everything went perfectly. I taught successful classes,
    my students praised me
    to my bosses, I was being requested.

I submitted a piece I was commissioned for
and the writer in question was pleased.
My poems were being published and praised.
I had been offered more work in the face of lockdowns
and a worldwide pandemic.
I knew I was lucky.

And then, as if that weren't enough,
one night I went outside, to the graveyard beside my
flat
– a still place I used a lot during lockdown –
to have a smoke. And then I saw a fox.

Not just saw one.

The fox stared at me, for a long time. She started
sniffing the graves nearby, running around in circles.
Whenever I moved my foot, she watched me. And
then, testing our connection, I walked away from her,
and she followed. She followed me halfway around the
graveyard and I stole amazed glances the whole way.
Then, she vanished into the darkness.

This was a sign. I don't know what, but I believe it was a sign.

After years of the world opening its ass and defecating,
some success, some peace, some happiness.

And then,

of course,

the next day,

I was terrified.

A knot twisted and coiled in my stomach.

My anxiety   came back, smiling

ever so brightly, like the Cheshire Cat.

The anxiety was here to say: 'Don't forget,

this can all vanish in a second.'

*　*　*

My anxiety and I met

when my father was diagnosed with cancer,

we spent months together

clawing on the edge of a diagnosis

or timeline,

every ping of the phone

every word uttered

every glance

could mean he had died.

The sick can die any day.

My anxiety pinned me down

from an ever-levitated state,

it made me understand that

my mind was a jumble sale

of half-formed things,

nothing is real in

limbo –

my anxiety would pinch me,

warn me,

whisper,

'You

are   not

OK.'

It was the only one to say it.

FATHER'S DAY
(& other dates)

Father's Day. That year – the first year of his death –
it was on the twenty-first of June.
After, I fled the UK in the hope
I could bury myself behind a pile of snow
disguised as a desk, that I could deal with my grief
on a date of my choosing,
a schedule death, grief and I
could agree upon. The month of November,
in Finland, there was a residency –
I wasn't aware of the trick:
The twelfth of November was Father's Day there.

*   *   *

In Australia it was the second of September, in Poland, the
twenty-third of June,
in Italy it was the nineteenth of March and in India, the
seventeenth of June.
I was reading *Revolutionary Road* on that day in June.
I remember the smell of sun against the attic ceiling,
my body warm as I sat in the desk chair my dad gave to me;
took it from work when he heard they were going to scrap it –
he hated waste. My fingers tucked between Yates' words,
turning to pages at random.
Richard Yates died on the seventh of November 1992.
I was born in 1992. The eighth of August.

*   *   *

My sister was born one week and four years before me: the first
of August 1988.
My mother was born on the twenty-third of December 1956.
My niece was born on the thirtieth of September 2008.
Vincent van Gogh was born on the thirtieth of March 1853,
Meryl Streep was born on
the twenty-second of June 1949, Aretha Franklin was born on
the twenty-fifth of March 1942, Diane Keaton was born on
the fifth of January 1946, Whoopi Goldberg was born on the
thirteenth of November 1955, Olivia Colman was born on the
thirtieth of January 1974.
My father was born on the twenty-third of October 1953.
Twenty-three was our number.

*   *   *

When I think about my father's birth I think about shabby
houses.
I think of my grandmother, sitting in an armchair with pink
cushions,
a memory I'm sure I made up. I think of my father's round nose
and the way he chewed his food, I remember the noises of it
and the smell of him in the morning. 1953, he came into this
world.
1953 was the year Arthur Miller's *The Crucible* opened on
Broadway,
it was the year of the North Sea flood, the year Ian Fleming
published
the first James Bond novel, it was the year of nuclear testing

and the coronation of a queen, the year they executed the
Rosenbergs
and Walt Disney's *Peter Pan* premiered.

*   *   *

Emily Brontë died on the nineteenth of December 1848, Lewis
Carroll died
on the fourteenth of January 1898, Judy Garland died on the
twenty-second of June 1969. Nina Simone died on the twenty-
first of April 2003. Lucille Clifton died on the thirteenth of
February 2010. Robin Williams died on the eleventh of August
2014. Two years before my father.
He died on the twenty-fifth of February. 2016. At 1.45 p.m.
　　　　It was a Thursday.

*   *   *

When I think about my father's death I think
about the sunlight
coming through the curtains, I think
of the carpet in the corridor, the sheets
and how they seemed to sag
because they knew what was coming
– I hide behind these domestic details –
it is easier to see. I cling to these dates,
for a moment of my choosing.

*   *   *

Father's Day starts in the supermarkets
a month early: cards come out addressed to *Dad*,
a selection of dad-appropriate gifts are clustered together
at the front of the store, so you can't forget.

The living will never understand the significance of this date,
only the dead and their shadows can know –
every day is Father's Day.

CRIB WITCH

When I crawled out
into this world,
my father sat on a beer-stained carpet
across the road.

I know that my grandfather
was the first to hold me
and cast a spell
in words around a fire.

My father found a witch
in his son's crib
when he arrived at the hospital –
yellow-fingered from cigarettes.

I remember him looking down at me,
among the miserable silent babies,
and I screamed at him, asked him
where he'd been, told him to never leave

again, and he didn't, beyond that night
for two decades he was there –
there is another version to this story
but I choose to see it this way –

even if he was just across the road,
he was there.

FAULT

'Your faults as a son is my failure as a father.'
– *Gladiator*

The best I can do
is pick you up from the ground

(wipe the sick from your eyes,
tears in your nose)

hold you, to see you as more
than a father,

just a boy, in a shell. I will
recognise you have offered what you can

and there always needs to be a first stone –
I will hold you tight, old man,

the man I will become.
The game is over

no you, no I
no them, no us.

I will say to you what we both know to be true:
that your faults as a father is my failure as a son.

A WISH

I wish there was a place
to find you

a stone to speak to

a tree to place flowers beneath

I wish we'd never burnt you
and put you
in a box

I wish I had you
to myself

I wish

I wish

BABADOOK

I.
Dad

This is a man you never knew
but heard of

he lived in whispered stories
and you in his gloom

because Mum won't talk about him
nor go down into the cellar:

All of your father's things are down there.

He's my father. You don't own him!

So you sneak down
wear his coat, shirt, hat,

if only to feel him,
to bring him back

to life and have him for yourself
to grow your own stories

to be able to say
I knew him.

11.
Mum

mum! your resentment is your
love your love is your resentment
your fear is your strength
pushing mum to the ground screaming

do you want *to die?*
she doesn't seem to get
this danger you're both wading in
guilt grief clamping tight

on the ground you can keep her
to protect her *mum!*
because you're terrified
of death of losing another one

mum! you were
born into a world
where death is not just possible
but plausible

mum! you won't let her sleep *mum!*
Because there's nothing more terrifying
than an unconscious *mum!*
You're totally alone in the world

when *mum's* asleep, when *mum's* alone

mum mum mum
you cannot protect her she cannot protect you
mumumumumumumumumumumum
and she is the only thing that matters

III.

Babadook

The Babadook is that shape
shadow hanging coat
shirt and hat
the shoes propped up against the skirting board

it's the unexplained noise
down the corridor the soft crackle
in the corner of the room – it's him
your dead husband dead father

that version of him you wanted to know
you invited him in, remember?
or just the memory you asked for
the ghost you always desired

the Babadook is grief laying in bed wanting
to sleep so numb dead everything's so loud
and quiet at the same time everyone's talking
about bullshit bullshit

and the Babadook is saying it's okay not to listen
because that noise in your head that numbness
is loud and all you can think of is death
death

but it's not really thinking it's sitting

in your mind just feeling it all move
stunned silent still
rageful deflated explosive pedantic
at the same time

screaming in the back seat
snapping at a stranger
because life is not life when there's someone missing
it is not the same life anyway

it's a horror movie
a genre you fell
into.

SIX BUTTERFLIES AND A MOTH ON A ROSE BRANCH

I see you, moth,
fluttering about
in that electric blur
at night,

I watch your strength
with every beat of your wing,
I watch you steadying yourself
within that frame,

you're an intruder, moth,
your heart beats
with your defiance, I see it
and know you have a weakness –

you are the moth
that walks over my grave,
that skates between
the hairs on my back

you are the moth
I've always wanted to ask questions
from the first time I saw you
hiding behind that portrait

I always wanted you to tell me a truth,
to show me what really goes on
in your head when you throw yourself

at my window – I always imagined

you had answers,
tell me something then, moth,
tell me something that used
to make me excited, tell me,

moth, which way it is
to the living
for I have lost
my way.

IN DEFENCE OF COMMODUS

I spend my life running from
        the man I'm cursed to be.

Commodus asks his dad,
        (with his rough, muddy hands
        his voice full of a life of being right)
why he doesn't love him. Says he's tried

so hard to like what dad likes,
        to be the boy he never was. Commodus
makes a case for himself, offering his value
        beyond that of swords and fists. I've never

been good with my fists. I was punched
        by a friend once, and what hurt most
        was not the sight of stars but the betrayal.

We feel nothing because we feel everything.

Shoving it down
        good little daddy-issued-volcanoes,
because that's what we've been taught to do.

And yet,
        even though that boy has been made
        of clay,
        without even realising, Commodus,

has one last plea,
      asks dad just to see him
to accept that what he has to offer
      is enough,

that kindness is not a weakness
that a poet is a Caesar. But dad,

that boy himself once,
cannot change, he too is made of clay

so Commodus crushes him, and takes his place.

ROAD TO PERDITION

the father has a father
has a father has a father
has his own issues
grudges anger crap
ghosts play bells
rain tingles falls chimes
bullet snaps light
men fall like sacks
piano kicks in shudders
the father is going to kill
the grandfather, father, son
glad it's you he says
the son picks up the gun
so simple necessary boom
killing that piece of you

ELFFIN AP GWYDDNO FINDS TALIESIN

My creations have always been flawed
but in their eyes I see souls. The gods have cruelly decided

that my children are not for this earth. I live in ellipsis.
My desire in life is very simple: I do not care

for crowns or kingdoms, I wish to be a father,
And yet I am without. For this is the only desire I have.

I will not raise my son to be a warrior,
or my daughter to be a wife. I will not tell part of the story

to my daughter and the other to my son –
I will tell them everything. They will make their own world

as I stand nearby, as I break the rules of fathers
and be something more. I will love and just love.

And in the lake, I find just that,
something that will become whatever it chooses to be.

EMPIRE OF DIRT

I look in the mirror
and see a stranger looking back;
maybe I see my father,
dead and young,
covered in pollen,
never dress him in yellow,
he said,
the bees will always come.

Don't dress me,
paint my skin
in a colour I do not recognise;
paint the answers to how
my desires are
not what they once were;
paint it in dirt,
run my rules in muck –
they've changed anyway,
throw my limits in the filth,
scrub my face in mud,

send me to the forest,
to a dark wood, to a land
of fallen leaves, to a cold cave
where I can scrawl my dreams
in blood and the sap of a tree,
where I'll rub dill into my wounds

and make music only the walls
engulf.

Send me to find a face
to win my body back;
pray
tell me that my body
will no longer lie mute, I remember it
like a child remembers its favourite food.
I know it exists,
this body of mine,
where I do not wake to that knock,
knock,
where I can simply be,
this is surely an existence that can occur,

so let me be
in the woods,
let me scream to the tallest tree
and find a fairy or a fool,
let me fall into that dirt
and smell the soil of my youth;
let me pull the flowers' roots
and plant them somewhere on the horizon, let me
tangle daisy-chains, so that I may pluck
each petal and ask if he loved me
or not.

This wood is my country,
my mother tongue, my climate,
if my body will no longer speak to me
let me place it in the belly of a tree
and barefoot I will walk on.

THIS NEW WORLD HAS THE SAME MOON

I didn't know what normal was
before it was taken away –

always planning the next thing,
my eye perpetually on the exit

thereby forgetting to be
here   now –

to stand beneath a tree
and watch a bird in its nest,

to drink the sun
greedily and unforgiving.

This new world has the same moon
but a different voice –

a soul that is being unearthed.
Mother, may we find some peace

and remember that hope
can be found beneath the tree with the bird.

In the kitchen talking to my mother,
hugging my niece and watching

her skate, it is me
here, writing this poem

it is everything before your fingers,
everything you cannot see.

MY FUNERAL

sometimes i crave a funeral
the last
was so long ago that
my allotted time
for grief
is up

youth is so fast
every day is a saturday
there's always a party roaring
rimming mandy weed & pizza
no one wants to talk about death
nor wants you
moon-face
sour puss
hurting

a funeral then
at a graveyard with grey clouds
like heavy eyelids
a gravestone with a name i know
with dates
i was only alive for some

and i'll stand hunched over silent
as the people walk away
i'll stand in my grief

here i will stand
here
i'll feel it all give in
grieve
here i will be
fucking miserable
not smile or talk

at funerals
i can be
me

BLUE

He was the only man
to call me blue,
the only man
who saw that pool
inside me,
saw me
wading through it
and knew.

PRYDERI

I heard my body's voice
after five years of absence
full of all the small things
it hadn't said

the sound of its words
rang like cove-water
and reminded me

how I choked it
into submission
abused my body
to the point of silence

but my body came back to me
and with it
my stomach lapped with old excitement –

no more fighting
no more violence

just us
finally talking
to one another.

HIS GRAVESTONE

we didn't give him a grave no place to put flowers

or a can of stella artois

no memoriam

so I can only hold him in my memory

in the cemetery shaped like sunken ships far from home

I stopped before one of a hundred stones

below his name the plaque read

                        we will know each other better when the mists
have cleared

and there I found him

NOTES & ACKNOWLEDGEMENTS

'Weekend' takes its name from, directly references and is inspired by Andrew Haigh's 2011 film of the same name. The lines '*straight people like us as long as we conform, we behave by their little rules / more proud than if I were the first man on the moon*' and '*let's not upset them, let's hide in our little ghettos, let's not hold hands, let's not kiss in the street, no*' are quotes from the film.

'Ivan the Terrible and His Son' is a response to and named after Ilya Repin's painting, *Ivan the Terrible and his Son Ivan on 16 November 1581* (painted between 1883–1885).

'Sister Act II' is a reworking of a quote from the 1993 film of the same name, directed by Bill Duke and written by Judi Ann Mason, James Orr and Jim Cruickshank.

The poem 'Babadook' takes its name from and directly references the 2014 film, *The Babadook*, directed and written by Jennifer Kent. The line '*He's my father, you don't own him*' is a quote from the film.

'In Defence of Commodus' references the 2000 film, *Gladiator*, directed by Ridley Scott and written by David Franzoni, John Logan and William Nicholson.

'Road to Perdition' is named after and references the 2002 film of the same name, directed by Sam Mendes. The screenplay was written by David Self and adapted from Max Allan Collins' graphic novel. The line '*glad it's you*' is a quote from the film.

'Prince Pwyll Visits His Son's Grave' is inspired by *The Four Branches of the Mabinogion*.

'Pryderi' is also inspired by *The Four Branches of the Mabinogion*. The word 'Pryderi' means 'care/worry' in Welsh.

'Elffin ap Gwyddno finds Taliesin' is a retelling of *The Hanes Taliesin*, a legendary account of the life of the poet Taliesin.

* * *

I want to give a huge thanks to the following publications.

'The Wizard of Oz', 'Cardiff Grindr, 2015' and 'Declaration' first appeared in my second poetry pamphlet, *Based on a True Story*, published by Fourteen Poems, 2021.

'The Men Who Wore Foxes on Their Heads', 'Poetic License', 'And Then the Flowers Came', 'There are Bees in My Beard', 'Empire of Dirt', 'Conkers', 'Real Boy', 'Sunflowers', 'Six Butterflies and a Moth on a Rose Branch' and 'Botanophobia' first appeared in my debut pamphlet, *Empire of Dirt*, published by Red Squirrel Press, 2019.

'This New World Has the Same Moon' was written for and performed at the Renfrewshire Arts Festival as part of the Scottish Mental Health Festival, 2021.

'My Anxiety Lives as an Acorn in My Stomach' was first published in the *Creating in Crisis* anthology, (Polari Press, 2021).

Parts of 'Weekend' and 'dead tooth' were first published in *ODD Mag*, 2021.

'Making Love to a Man' was first published in *Poetry Wales*, 2021.

'Road to Perdition' was first published in *The Glasgow Review of Books*, 2019.

* * *

Eileen Myles said that in every poetry book there is the book that didn't make it; the poems that didn't quite work, the ideas better suited elsewhere. This is true for me. Drafts flooded my flat as I wrote this book and there are a litany of people who gave their help.

I'd like to start by thanking everyone at Polygon, especially Edward Crossan, thank you for taking such time and care whilst editing this book.

To the Scottish Book Trust, for granting me a New Writers Award, which gave me the time and money to finally finish this project. In addition, to everyone at Moniack Mhor for making my stay tranquil and a perfect place to think and be and write. To Claire Askew, my mentor as part of the award, whose guidance, understanding and commitment to my work was unparalleled. I couldn't have asked for a better mentor, thank you.

To all my teachers at the Universities of Warwick and South Wales; Philip Gross, David Morley, Tim Parks, Tiffany Murray, Catherine Merriman, Barrie Llywelyn.

To my fellow poets, Anne Hay and Olive Ritch, who read some of these poems in their early stages and were generous with their feedback. To those that have championed my work through the years, Andrew McMillan, Ben Townley Canning and Sheila Wakefield.

To all my friends, I love you and I thank you for being with me along the journey.

To Yannick, for all your kindness and love, and the many hours you spent shuffling the poems around on the floor with me. I'm very lucky to have you.

To my family, those that are still with me – my mother, Carol Stewart, my sister, Jen, my niece, Amelia, Aunty Jan and Aunty Chris.

And to those that are no longer with us – my grandmother, Linda Whelan, my grandfather, John Terrance Whelan and my father, James Gordon Stewart. This is for you, Dad. This is our story.